PROCUREMENT STORIES
By Bruno Alvarez

Procurement Stories

Second Edition Guatemala: March, 2015

First Edition 2014, Bruno Alvarez
All rights reserved
Guatemala City, Guatemala

www.procurementstories.com

Any comments about this edition and content can be made to:
Bruno.a.alvarez@gmail.com

*This book is dedicated to all the
Contracting and Procurement
professionals
Who are working hard on adding
value
to their organization.*

During my professional career I encountered many anecdotes that translated later on in learning opportunities. Some gave a pretty good insight in the dos and don'ts of my profession. Being in the Contracting and procurement function it gave a pretty good set of both enlightening and entertaining stories that I collected in the past few years. This book is a collection of eighteen of such stories. The objective is to entertain the casual reader as well as teach a lesson or two to the procurement professional.

About the second Edition

Many mayor events occur during the year 2014 both global in the business world and in my life. On this second edition I review the current events and give a perspective from the Sourcing, Contracting and procurement function. Sometimes we neglect to see current events from this perspective and loose on the insight we can capture from this view. This edition has this events sorted next to some of the first edition stories so relevant topics are mixed and match. Sure to delight the strategic sourcing and procurement professional.

WHERE IT ALL BEGINS

Being working for some twenty years in the contracting and procurement function in top fortune 100 companies I have seen many many things. Things that will make you laugh, cry, inspire and, make you think. It has always strike me how the contracting and procurement function is as strategic as other functions but still it is not well understood and embraced in many corporations. A few years ago, no more than five or ten it became regarded as a strategic edge in business. Mostly it is well accounted for in global top quartile companies but not on the ground companies.

I remember a comment in a group discussion on a procurement manager answer to a young buyer´s question: why don't we get hefty commission or public recognition like the sales guys? The answer: there is no glamour in purchasing! Go back to your cubicle!

Even the semantics, some people would have problem describing what procurement means. In my current role my team is part of the Supply Chain department and people call us "compras" which means from Spanish both purchasing and shopping. I get the occasional comment: so you get paid to go shopping?

One day after realizing how the world, or at least the business world, would be a better place with the understanding of the procurement function, I set out to educate on the subject. Definitely there are many channels and the blog is a great one. My idea is to share stories and hopefully we can all together learn from them and have a little entertainment in the process.

LIKE IT OR NOT YOU OWN THE CATEGORY. THE STORY OF THE CAR AS A BENEFIT (CAB)

Like it or not when you get assigned a category as a category manager in a Contracting, sourcing and procurement department, you take on a child of your own, and anything and everything about this category will affect you directly. Let me explain with a story. Although I was not the one assigned to the category I sat right next to the guy that did. He got the sourcing of the light vehicles. Being in a fuel company with the main business being a retail operation; must of the light vehicles fell into two categories: The JAC which was the job allocated car and the CAB the car as a benefit vehicle. The JAC is very straight forward you get a vehicle that will help you do your job. Most of the JAC cases where sales staff visiting retail sites in a geographical regions, or rugged vehicles used on the plants that will travel from the coast to the city. The CAB was a whole different story altogether. The vehicle was a benefit and this meant for some manager having a vehicle that will describe their successful career, a vehicle that will represent their hierarchy and many felt they should have an opinion on the scope of the vehicles to be purchased.

My neighbor category manager got a complicated task for the CAB vehicles. See at first it was very simple because a global category manager decided to buy the CAB vehicles together for the whole Latin America region. Good move! Got a good discount with the volume and a very good deal all together. So good of a deal that the vehicles got really crafty upgrades. A brand new fleet of Volkswagen Jetta sports sedans with an upgraded 1.8 Turbo engine and other nice features got shipped to all Latin American sites. Everybody was thrilled, managers, human resources even the category manager in charge. He practically just did the procurement of getting the fleet into the country and the local support, all good. Well that was until the first vehicle got stolen some six months later. Before the end of the year another three got stolen. After eighteen months eight out of the twenty two got stolen. So it happens that nice popular cars like those where specially sought by the car thieves. The more popular the car the more prone to be stolen. What a nightmare! The risk management decided to change the cars immediately! But a big question was raised: what car should we source? Well find out what the least attractive cars for thieves and get those. The problem is that the cars least attractive for thieves are the ones that are what we called a bad purchase. High total cost of ownership, low aftermarket prices, no local representatives, shortage of spare parts, not the most popular in terms of looks and popularity. Remember this are the CABs managers will definitely rally up. Still my neighbor had to follow orders and got a deal for the cars to be exchanged for the one he identified as the least attractive car for thieves based on insurance statistical data. The winner a Renault Megane sedan. Pretty nice car but not too popular in the country. Managers did not like it but it was better than having yourself killed over a car.

For a while everything calm down. Theory was right the cars did not get stolen. Still the managers where not happy. This is where the category manager learned how the category will own him. They had all kinds of trouble with the cars. They will end up at the shop all the time because of all kinds of issues. The category manager will intervene most of the time and will spend most of his time pampering the managers' issues. From AC's broken down to dented body parts to lost keys. I saw the parade of people coming to his desk! On the top list I remember one calling with the following statement: The cars are really bad, I was passing a truck on a curve in a hill and the car stalled! I could have had an accident! I thought to myself: WHAT! Are you serious!! What were you thinking passing a truck in a curve on a hill to begin with!!! The best one came when one manager came stumping his feet furious: The keys to the cars are all the same and someone mistakenly took my car!! Again I thought to myself: What! Ok come down I said. He rambled on and on that someone took his car by mistake. Then he called another manager in front of us: You have the same color as mine so you probably took my car! At this time I´m thinking: this guy is nuts! Obviously the other manager said: mmm nope, this is not your car. We decided to go down to the parking lot to check for the car. So it happened he parked on the third level and he was looking for the car on the second level. All levels are identical. The car was sitting there. If the car had reactions it will probably will be laughing its tailpipe off.

So at the end my next office neighbor category manager will bear with all the vehicle troubles for this is his category. So source with that in mind so you can keep the company and yourself out of future troubles.

SAVE SMART

Sometimes a sales slump or a cash flow crunch pushes a company into savings mode. Once I was in a brainstorm meeting to see where we could save some money. Went for a second to the bathroom and to my amazement all the bathroom products where replaced by lower quality ones. The soap dispenser was different it had a very simple underperforming hand soap. The paper towels where smaller and very rough and the toilet paper was so thin you could see through.

I went back to the meeting and the facilities manager said "we are already taking measures to save!" it holds true that a penny saved is a penny earn but then again you only save pennies. If you want to succeed in saving money to your business start by performing a spend analysis. Take a, tops down approach, and look at your top spending categories. Find the main categories and work hard at them.

It is true as it does with many cases that your top twenty percent categories hold the top eighty percent spend. So find that top categories and spend your time and efforts on them. Develop strategies, implement them and follow through until you get the best results possible. Don´t go messing with the office supplies that will only demoralize your employees.

SAVED 40% WHEN 3% WAS ASPIRATIONAL, HOW DID THAT HAPPENED?

Sitting on my desk on a June morning back in 2011, I get a call from the regional CPO. I'm looking at the savings report from Central America, it says here that you guys already met your target since February? Yes sir. You are 130% on your bottom line savings in my midyear review report. Yes we are. There must be a mistake or something, it says here that a single negotiation that saved 40% on a one million purchase on February. That is probably wrong. Mmmmm, nope.

Well I went to look at the budget and it was 6 mayor parts for generation engines that are custom made to order, machined specifically for us. As I went back, we buy this every year and have managed to save by really tough negotiations a 3% when we have volume, so there is definitely a mistake here. No sir there is no mistake, we manage to save 40% this time. Well I asked your boss the Central America purchasing manager and he could not explain to me (CPO) so he said to talk directly to you. Explain before I delete this transaction from the report and will need evidence of whatever you're going to say. At this point I was impressed by the lack of confidence from my superiors, but still, I had the answer.

Well I talked to the sales director for Americas and asked a straight forward question: What is the main driver in the cost of this parts? I thought it was the material, but the answer, I was not expecting at all: well to tell you the truth is my shop time. I have too many orders of this parts and I have to outsource very costly on other shops, they have to be very specialized. If I wait more for the delivery then will it be cheaper? The answer was YES! So I asked them to give me a quote for different deliveries against discount and went to our plant to check when this parts were needed.

To my luck they were needed by the end of the year. The discount went from 10% for 60 days up to 40% for 180 days.....plenty of time. Closed the deal 40% off a one million dollar purchase, cover the 400K USD savings target… all good!
The CPO got the proposal I received and did not hear from him for a while, but at the end of the year he was recognized for the savings efforts in the region so I guess he was more than satisfied.

A WORD ON INCOTERMS

Once I found myself buying a set of large electro-mechanical valves custom made for a specific application. The vendor was from the US but had a representative in Costa Rica. Since this where going to Guatemala the Rep was the closest to the final destination. They originally quoted me EX-Works a US warehouse.

Since the sales rep was relatively close I told him: Can you do DDU? He automatically freaked out. He started shooting mails to all his technical support team. The mails went something like this: They are asking me for a DDU! does the valves include a DDU? Do we sell our valves with DDU? Where does a DDU go in a valve? And what is the function of a DDU? After the "Boss" abruptly stopped the mails with a quote from the internet with the incoterm definition of Delivered Duties Unpaid (DDU).

When doing purchasing of international goods there is not enough double checking on what the incoterm means EXACTLY. Make sure you understand completely what the term means and the responsibility it defines. This is where your vendor ends and you begin. Don´t take it lightly.

THE WIN – WIN ILLUSION

A buyer went out to rent a crane for a job that will take more or less 6 months. He went to our usual negotiated provider. He quoted some 5,000 USD for the month plus this and that for mobilization and others. There were some 6 different models available that could do the job but the construction team had the eye on one in particular.

It might do the job in less time but this was not for sure. When the buyer went to ask for the preference, the vendor asked for an additional 1,000 USD for the right to chose. The buyer discourage went back and informed. He negotiated back and forth with the vendor and the construction team until they reached an agreed 450 USD for the right to pick. He said how about the Win – Win negotiation I just did!

Well that to me is more of a Lose – Lose situation. True Win – Win negotiations are the ones that have very few, or none at all, concessions. The more you grant the more you move to a, lose – lose, lose – win or win – lose outcome. Two things to consider, one is that the higher the complexity and the value the more key points to negotiate and it become more of a game of concessions.

The other to consider is the relationship level. If you are negotiating a one time or one off go for the Gold, but if not, remember to look at the forest and not the tree. If you will be negotiating with this vendor in the future be careful no to set yourself a trap along the road.

PROCUREMENT IN SMALL MARKETS, DON´T GET HIT BY A CAR?!

In one of the smallest countries in Central America I had the chance to talk with a maintenance manager. He would be in charge of purchasing all the spare parts for the maintenance of a fast food chain for all equipment. Most of his duties will be getting a spare parts inventory of the usual parts and will buy from the local distributors. From time to time some main equipment will be replaced and during the year he would get to buy equipment worth a procurement process with spend above 10K USD.

I asked him about his process. "I will usually ask for proposal from the two main local suppliers, then I will negotiate back and forth with them until I get the best price" I then asked, what would prevent you to negotiate back and forth with the two? The answers was something I wasn´t expecting at all: "well the only thing that will prevent me from negotiating back and forth is getting hit by a car!" excuse me... could you explain?? "Well see the two local representatives have their warehouse one block from mine and they sit in front of each other across the street. I will ask for the price of the equipment, then I will cross the street and ask the other for a better price, I will do this until no discount is applied anymore!" no words could explain what I felt and thought... I went to the door and looked outside, saw the two signs one across the street from each other and half a block away.

Later that day when the shift was over they asked me to accompany them for some afternoon beers, I wanted to go back to the hotel so I passed. Had to wait for almost an hour for the taxi, everyone else left. When I finally left I passed in front of the two vendors and I though "Them two vendors and the manager must be all having beers on the other corner together!"

This little anecdote reminded me of how fragile and complicated small markets can be. A lot of attention must be put to the offering and thinking out of the box is not only good it is mandatory. I´ve seen in many cases that the best solutions come from expanding the market and moving it out of the "small" class.

TIME IS A RESOURCE AND AN ASSET

Every time I encounter a contract to be review because it will expire, or it just needs a review, time becomes the center of attention. Independently of what the best strategy might be, it seems that Time becomes highly relevant. Most cases Time is not enough to conduct a full procurement process. Usually there is a lot of pressure to have a contract in place by a certain date.

Procurement is a function that has to manage well time. It is a very important competence for a buyer, senior buyer, contract manager, category manager or procurement manager. If your process is not schedule you are bound to fail. Stakeholder engagement is all about actions and scheduling. Time is directly proportional to results in procurement.

Many times management and vendors/contractors will highly appreciate realistic goals including the execution time and schedule than wishful thinking. Once, a project manager, approach a machine shop and said "I want it built in half the time!" "We can save some time here and there, but still, if you want it done in half the time, we will have to just give it to you half finished".

Recommendations: Plan ahead, have a plan in place, have a realistic schedule, engage everybody involved.

LAST MINUTE CAPITAL EXPENSE, A RACE TO SPEND!

On a sunny day in the last week of September, I get into a meeting with the capex project team. They had a grueling meeting the day before that started in the afternoon and ended late at night. You can sense in the team all the marks left by stress, exhaustion and lots of caffeine. The meeting is between us, the contracting and procurement team, and the capex project team; what about? Capex execution. A very worn out capex team leader opened up the meeting with the following remarks: We have only spent twenty percent of the capital expense budget and taking into account the works programmed during the last quarter of the year we have only thirty three of the total capex! We stayed all night yesterday figuring out how to spend the other seventy percent and we are going to need your help in expediting the sourcing process. My first reaction is: How can this be happening again! I don´t mean because it happened last year and the year before, I´ve seen it happened all the time in many different companies.

I went and dissected how the contracting and procurement function provides a sourcing service but has the mission to do it strategically so the business can get a competitive advantage. I went through the sourcing process and how neglecting steps can cause serious harm both to the bottom line and even to the health and security of employees. I got back from the team an explanation of how not implementing the capex will cost a whole lot of money and that financially asking for money for a project and then not executing it is a financial suicide. This discussion can go on forever if you let it. As I have experienced before a "in the middle" solution is sough and implemented.

How did this shortcoming of time to spend capex happens in the first place? How did the capex project team end up at the end of the third quarter with only twenty percent of spend execution? Why does this keep repeating itself? There might be a number of reasons, the reason I´ve seen as the most common is OVERPLANNING. Yes sounds crazy but is the main reason I´ve have encountered, and believe me I´ve seen this phenomenon too many times. The Capex team plans carefully, a year before, on the projects they want to implement. They prepare elaborate business cases that go under deep scrutiny. The investment is accurately revised and execution plan goes along with the plan. All good in this stage. Then the year begins and everybody starts the projects. Actually starting the projects is where time is spent that can move a project from week one to week thirty two. Getting the "right moment" can also lag the project. Also many projects are half-approved and need to complete some hurdle to be completely approved. Other time there is a lack of human resources to execute. The worst one is just plain old procrastination on the part of the implementing team.

Don´t get me wrong there are cases where a project is right on budget and execution wise. For the ones that do not happen timely expect to waste good old money on expediting cost and poor strategic planning. Contracting and Procurement can do both fast and expensive or timely and strategically on the later creating a competitive advantage for the business. Is a matter of choice!

SUPPLIER RELATIONSHIP MANAGEMENT AND TRUST

As the discipline calls it is a relationship and that encompass all related to one. One of its components is trust. A couple of months ago a friend got into a business relationship with an informal car washer. He would always complain that when he got his car washed and it rained the same day, he should get his money back. He convinced the car washer to discount one car wash if the same day rained. He hardly knew the washers name, where he washed cars, and how big his business was. The washer only talked with him when he went to get his payment.

As you might guess by now the inevitable happened. There was a tropical storm and it rained for several days in a row. The Car Washer never showed up again.

A good relationship includes communication and trust. Your suppliers are a key part of the business if they fail you, your whole operations fails. There is a need to build a relationship with communication and trust. Take the time to understand how they operate, what the main drivers are, and how it affects the overall performance.

Once a communication channel has being established you should be the first to be informing on issues that will affect you as a client, just as if you were part of the suppliers' management team. At the end you partner with your supplier so treat them as such.

REPORTING SAVINGS, THE GOOD THE BAD AND THE UGLY

As the end of the year approaches, it's time to check the different savings initiatives. I was going through our Latin America region and one project caught my attention. A 12.5 million work on a generation turbine. The team was reporting a 10 plus million dollar savings.

Ok guys, how could that happened? Well we are not going to do the repair because it was determined that it is not necessary. What did we do with the other 2.5 million? Well we spend it doing the preliminary assessment on the equipment. Probably any CPO reports something like this and gets his head chopped off in the board meeting.

Kind of reminded me when I was at a capex meeting analyzing potential savings initiatives and through a comment as a joke: Out of these 2 million dollars we have in capex I know how to save 1 Million! We just buy half of everything! Reporting savings is tricky.

The GOOD when you have a legitimate indicative and you save a good amount due to a well-executed procurement strategy.

The BAD when you have no indicative and whatever you report will be questionable even though it might be true.

The UGLY is when you try so hard just to "report" big savings that you skew the perceptions and report unbelievable things. Just like a time bomb it will blow up in your face sooner or later.

GREAT PROCUREMENT IS NOT JUST RUNNING A BIDDING EVENT

I just came out of a contracting process for a completely new commodity. The process was a first try at purchasing this commodity and the result was regarded as "A Complete Success" by the stakeholders.

Our next natural step is to go out and get a term contract. Ok, we have a good feel of the market, we got a good insight on the business needs and we got a peep at a contract structure. All of the sudden I get a request that threw me off. Can you please train this junior member of the accounting staff in how to use our e-sourcing tool? What are you thinking? We want for him to take care of the term contract. I felt like I was falling from a cliff! You mean when we get to the part where we execute the strategy? No since we did the spot purchase we only need to invite the same vendors to a term contract bidding event! We get our lawyers to prepare a template contract and that´s all! Ok now I´m falling from a cliff!

The Procurement process in a nut shell goes through: Business needs, Market Analysis, Defining strategy, Executing strategy, Award, Contract. Neglect any of the steps and you are in deep trouble. So how did my stakeholders come up with a single step? Simple "VISIBILITY" like the iceberg that sunk the titanic, they only see the bidding event. They were involved on all steps but they thought that the bidding event was the main event. Also the e-sourcing tool makes them believe that the event can be set up like a recipe.

 I will have to review the procurement process with my stakeholders before the "next steps" or else, we surely have them scratching their head wondering what went wrong.

LEADERSHIP IN PROCUREMENT

Found myself at a contract renewal of third party labor. A very open discussion began of the performance of the previous contract. The performance was very poor, and the discussion was around what was needed to improve it. The curious thing is that this contract assembled almost all departments. Plant operations are the main stakeholders but they needed the support from human resources. Legal had a big part because of labor laws and restrictions. Also finance had a word due to payment methods and even the safety guys because the labor will work at a plant where proper safety measures need to be follow at all time. This meeting involved some 15 to 20 people at a time.

This situation made me think that procurement is a leadership intense discipline. Went to read some about leadership and got a strong impression that all recommendations where around the leader and the leader traits. The best information found was that leadership is effective when you focus on the people that need to be lead, and not centric on the leader.

This approach is about getting the job done though people. Put the lead by leading people plan to action and it proved to be a sweet success. By placing focus on people and the proper follow up, the contract renewal became like an orchestra that played a well-crafted tune!

THE WORLD IS COMING TO BRAZIL, HOW DO YOU HANDLE THE LOGISTICS?

The FIFA World Cup has a significant impact in global economy. Having 204 countries as members and 3.6 billion viewers it is most definitely a global "big business". Expected a visit of at least 600,000 tourist plus 3 million Brazilian as local tourism and adding a whopping $70 billion to the Brazilian economy. How about jobs, 332,000 permanent jobs and 381,000 temporary jobs. Knowing this numbers it makes me ponder on the logistics needed. Some of the basics are high quality procurement, sourcing and delivery.

How to come about such a great feat? Nothing can go wrong since the event is so short, a little over a month. To meet the needs an expression comes to my mind used for this kind of cases: "how do you eat an elephant, one bite at a time!" This kind of works needs to be broken in thousands of smaller jobs over a period of time. Since the size of this event is so colossal it will take a significant amount of time and man hours. No wonder the drawn has being made for the 2018 and 2022 games. The host countries will need such time to get ready.

Besides breaking up the task into little smaller jobs also good planning has to be placed. There is a dedicated team in charge of planning each individual job and a good set of planners, schedulers and the sort all orchestrated in different levels of command. A great global industrial big business in deed.

When you come across a large procurement/sourcing project remember the learning that comes from this spectacular global event. Break the project into smaller ones, until you are comfortable with the size of each. Get them down to "doable" smaller projects. Set up a schedule

and start to eat your own elephant
one bite at a time!

THE BIRTH OF A BRAND LOGO

Recently I participated as a guest speaker for the 20th Annual Coal Conference of the Americas organized by IHS McClosky in Cartagena, Colombia. Being in the Energy and Oil industry sector I've attended several of such conferences, but as a guest speaker, this is a first for me. I have lecture for a while and I've being invited as a guest speaker to some events, but none of this magnitude. All the experts are at hand, all the commercial teams from the main coal providers and all the major coal consumers are present.

It began back in October 2012 where I was contacted by a correspondent of IHS McClosky for an invitation as a Gust Speaker. This was the second time I have being invited but the company that I currently work for does not endorse this type of participation. I expressed this issue in the past and again on October last year. I suggested that I could participate as an Independent Consultant and, if the company I work for is not mention, they will be OK with my participation.

On March the 12th, I was on a plane to Cartagena. Couple of days prior to the conference I came across that I had no business cards with my name only as an Independent Consultant. My wife who is an Architect does all the graphic design for herself and in my household. She made a really nice design for the cards. All of the sudden I realized I had no brand logo. As important as it is to have a recognizable graphic representation, I had none.

We tried different things, Random shapes, Free form, Different letter combinations, natural forms and none seem to work. I did some soul searching and realized it´s all about meaning, representing what you are.

After a really cool moment of truth, I came up with my new Brand Logo (see image).

Some ten years ago I got involved in the Oil industry with a top Quartile Company. They had the best contracting and procurement function. They taught me so much and for that I´m forever grateful.

One of the concepts that stroke me the most was the duality of the purchasing process. There is a Strategic side of it and an operational one. The strategic concentrates on Value Improvement while the Operational concentrates on buying efficiency.

Some while back it was discovered that the Pareto Principle would apply to this process too. The top 20% of transactions will represent the 80% of the spend and likewise the 80% of your transactions will represent 20% of your spend. When you apply this to the purchasing function you get that the top 80% of your spend are strategic and the bottom 20% of your spend is operational purchasing with a lot of transactions. I needed to explain this very often so did my teammates in contracting and procurement.

I came up with a graphic representation of this concept with two balls and two arrows and a line between them.

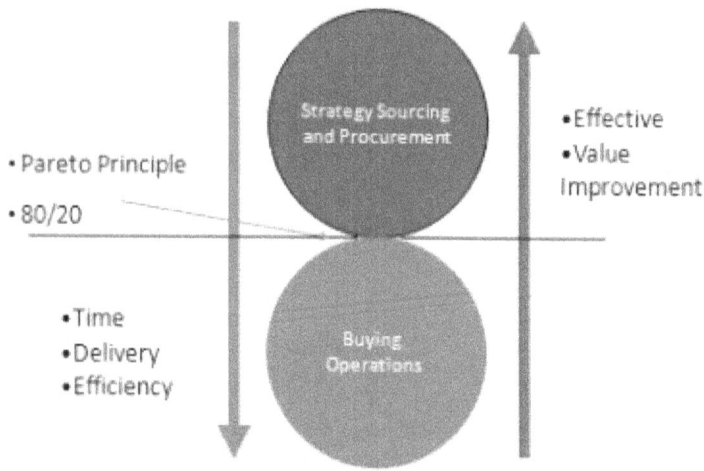

The top Ball is the strategic purchasing and the bottom ball the operational purchasing. The arrows represent the tops- down and bottoms-up approach respectively. The lines between the two balls, represents the 80/20 spend break point.

This representation became widely used in Contracting and procurement; my friends will call it Bruno´s balls as a joke I prefer "B" principle. So what better for my brand logo as an Independent Contracting and Procurement Consultant!

WHY IS THE COAL DEMAND GROWING IN CENTRAL AMERICA? DON'T FORGET THE TOTAL COST OF OWNERSHIP AND THE SUPPLY CHAIN.

While in North America the Coal is being replaced by other fuels like Natural Gas, in Countries like Guatemala, Honduras and Panama is the opposite. Coal fired plants are being built in Central America and by the year 2015 the demand for thermal coal will almost triple.

How does this happen in two regions so near? Cost is the main driver in the power generation industry in both cases? The answer is pretty simple indeed: Total Cost of ownership. (TCO) In northern American countries there is indigenous Gas, it´s already there somehow. If you look at the supply chain there are few links and that means lower cost.

Another answer that complements the question is The Market; if you study the global market trends Gas is on the cheap. If cost is your driver and when I say cost is TCO then it makes sense to turn to Gas if you are in the northern hemisphere of the American continent. That said when you look at Central America that uses a lot of bunker fuel; it only makes sense to replace this fuel by a cheaper TCO one.

There is no indigenous Gas so when you analyze the Supply Chain Cost it actually is cheaper on a TCO basis The Coal over Gas and Bunker. Put the market into perspective and you see lower Coal prices due to lower coal demand in the rest of the world.

The result: new plants being built that will replace old bunker fuel engines and that will cope with future demand. It is interesting to see that the landed cost of fuels in Central America is made up by 25% the cost of the fuel at the source, and 75% is the transport, handling and other expenses.

If you miss to analyze your Supply Chain and then understand the Total Cost, you will fail at your procurement efforts on savings and cost effectiveness.

THE ONE MISTAKE YOU CAN'T AFFORD IN A NEGOTIATION

On a recent contract initiative I saw the mistake that cannot be accepted in negotiations. You might get away with missed calls on small concessions, paying a bit over the market or missing a detail that has small impact but you can't miss on this one.

The contract initiative was about buying commodities for consumption. This commodity needs some level of understanding of the global market, commodity markets and other factors. Index pricing is also a must, and how this index is specified. Saw how a team neglected to prepare for a negotiation heavy on market intelligence. The result, well, the provider did a tap number on that contract. In the contract it was purposely referred to an index that referred to a different market, as you might guess, higher prices.

Lots of money will be overpaid in the next twelve months. By now you are wondering what the unaffordable mistakes is: (drum roll) DO YOUR HOMEWORK! Yes! Prepare for a negotiation with all the information available and then, some more! All the team members have to know all there is to know about the main objectives, drives and your counterpart.

A lot has being written about negotiating skills but that will be phase two, if you don't prepare there is no skill that is worth using in a negotiation. So if you don't want to be in the "lose" of a "win-lose" negotiation, do one thing before anything, be prepared!

FIVE TIPS FOR EFFECTIVE, PRODUCTIVE MEETINGS

So many times I come into a meeting with high expectations, only to come out frustrated because the time invested was not what I wished for. The usual thoughts go through my mind, the different more productive things we could all be doing, or, the back tracked task on my to do list. That said I´m the type of person that likes to take action when there is something that I do not like or does not click. For that reason I took into the task of interviewing many people, especially people I know are well respected for being organized and have good grasp of the value of time. From that input here are five tips for effective, productive meetings, hope this brings value to your everyday activities.

Tip 1: Short and Sweet! Plan to hit the few main points. Don´t try to squeeze too many topics in one meeting agenda. Keep them half an hour, or an hour at the most. Longer meetings most definitely keep the attendants from paying attention.

Tip 2: Prepare Beforehand! Plan your agenda, get all the audio video equipment ready and have all the involved informed. Send pre-reading material if necessary and don´t forget to include the entire incumbent. Be at the meeting room five to ten minutes before the set time.

Tip 3: Create an Agenda and Stick to it! Don´t come into a meeting with no agenda or just a vague idea. Have a clear list of matter to address .If conversations start to come off track, correct the course and if necessary set a new meeting for off agenda topics that need to be address as well.

Tip 4: No distractions! All computers and smart phones should be off. Let´s face it; no human can actively participate in a meeting and answer mails and messages at the same time and yield the best they can to either one. It tends to go to tip 1 if you keep them short and sweet there is no need for people to be connected intensively during the meeting.

Tip 5: Don't create a collaborative document in a meeting! If you are to create a new document don´t create meetings for this. Produce a draft of the document, and then have them all look at this draft and elaborate on this rough idea. When the draft has gone to extensive individual review then a meeting can take place to discuss. Creating documents in meetings from scratch is a big investment in time.

NOW NOBODY WANTS TO MANAGE THE CONTRACT!

Big mistake is to form a team, multi-functional team made up of a variety of department and functions and do not prepare a roles and responsibilities matrix on the management of the contract. Lately I saw how a contract was procured very nicely with a very broad team, when the time to management came, nobody wanted the responsibility! See this team did not prepare roles for the contract management.

Since this contract is very important for the overall operation of a plant the obvious was for the operations team to manage the execution of the contract. The issue began when they wanted to manage the contract but wanted to avoid responsibility if something fails. Nice try guys! The usual happened, endorse all responsibility to the guys that did the procurement! To make things go west, the Legal team started to try and decide what, who and when, yes you read it right, the legal team! To make a long story short the argument still on the table of the team!

Lesson to be learned here, set up your contract management plan with a clear definition of roles and responsibilities and remember the procurement guy is responsible to add value, the stakeholders to manage the contract.

IS THERE A LESSON TO BE LEARNED IN THE DISAPPEARING OF MALAYSIAN AIRLINES FLIGHT MH370 IN CONTRACTING AND PROCUREMENT?

Last August I went to Kuala Lumpur to dictate a course on Procurement Best Practices. On my way back to Guatemala I took a flight very similar to the MH370 flight, only mine went from Kuala Lumpur to Hong Kong. When I heard the news I was shocked! I had the feeling of: it could have been me! Then the sentiment for the family dug deep within me. I´ve being following the news very closely and feel deeply for the families of those 239 passengers still missing. Going back in my mind sitting in that large plane all I can think is how this huge plane can go missing! We are living in a communication boom nothing is a mystery and all information is available in a fraction of a second! And still we are over a month later still searching. Still with that void within, I decided to go about and see how I can contribute, how everybody can contribute so that this should not happen again. How to contribute from my perspective, well, I gather my procurement team and brainstormed how in an operation our procurement function could have contribute to avoid such mishap?

To answer this question we rambled for a while on different ideas, we look at historic cases of planes gone missing, and, after all that, a common theme boiled to the top. If some mechanical failure is to be associated with this event, then something might of being done, that was not the best solution, probably a cutting cost initiative that was not done correctly, often neglecting the contribution of the procurement team. When cutting cost ends in lowering quality, this things tend to happen. When I say quality I not only mean in materials, it can be service too or even vendor quality which is reflected in inconsistency of their deliveries.

There's a lot to be said on how this uneducated impulse cost savings initiatives can cause harm.

Moving forward, how can we avoid such failures? Well the answer is simpler that what you might think. Instead of lowering cost with lowering quality go for the gold! Get the best solution and improve its cost to match the other lower cost offerings! Don't settle for less than the best, and get the cost right! Procurement is a function set up to add value not just to lower cost. Get the right specifications and then work on the best cost. This adds value!

IF YOU DON´T KNOW WHERE YOU ARE GOING ANY BUS WILL TAKE YOU THERE...E-SOURCING AND TOOLS OF THE TRADE

I found myself in yet another roll out of a procurement suite to support the procurement function. After a couple of this implementations, I have come to learn how there are big expectations and high promises of success. This tools are really good.

They have evolved into this fully integrated set of support tools that go from sourcing, to spend analysis, and really advanced market intelligence and decision support functionalities. Most of the tools have integrated best practice so you cannot miss the mark. For a while I have been using this tools and the first thing that comes to my mind is "don´t forget the procurement itself!" Yes, this new tools, for the new and inexperienced, may lure them into just go and use the tool and forget about the work that has to be done.

Let me explain, if you want a nail on the wall you will do nothing with your bare hand, you need the tool, the hammer. But still using the hammer needs skills, if you hit the nail in the wrong way you will have a crocked nail or do nothing. Also before even you begin you need to do your homework on what type of nail you need, size, material, etc. and the right hammer for the job. That said; is the same for procurement and the tools.

You need to prepare your procurement process from business needs to market analysis, supply chain modeling and strategy selection. Fail to do so will end up in a bad execution of your procurement and will probably blame the tools.

So if you plan to hang something on the wall or need to procure a multimillion key contract you need to do your process, tools are just aids to get the work done.

WHAT WOULD BE A GOOD KPI SET FOR A NEW PROCUREMENT DEPARTMENT?

Recently I posted this question on a very dynamic procurement oriented group in Linked-in. I was looking to create a new set of KPI for an organization that has recently come on board of strategic Sourcing. For a couple of decades this company has had tremendous success in its industry and now they are looking into the future. Most of the procurement has being done intuitively but now they set out to organize a contracting and procurement department or to be more specific a strategic sourcing department. I thought of the usual Spend based KPI's: savings, plan against actual, spend procured out of the total Spend. Procurement function cost against plan. But what else should be measured on the first year of a Young department?

I was overwhelmed with responses from the discussion group. I received Very good responses on what to focus on the first year, great advice and really creative KPI. The main takeaway from all the experts that contributed was the following:

Basically do three things to create a good KPI set for this new Procurement department within a traditional business that did only basic purchasing before:

1. Spend based KPI
2. Align KPI with the business objectives.
3. Assess the business expectation on the new procurement department.

Besides that I decided to do an extended dashboard with more metrics (not necessarily KPI) that will help me steer my function and give me visibility.

The main takeaway is to understand what is expected from your department by your management, shareholders and stakeholders. Understand also the business objectives. After that all is left, is to steer the ship!

TEN PROCUREMENT DO´S AND DON´TS

When it comes to dos and don'ts a lot falls into common sense, still it is always good to run down a list to help spark a good and healthy thought process. From all functions there are good practices and basic things that might be obvious, but still, we see trouble lurking in the future when we fail to consider this practices. On this list I tried to skip familiar good practices like time management, good communication and the like, and tried to focus on more procurement specific recommendations. Hope you find this nurturing and, if things go well, a good thought process will be provoked to improve your everyday activities.

Do:

> 1. Always engage your stakeholders and keep them informed.

2. Have a clear understanding of the scope of the category you aim to procure.

3. Keep your sourcing process fair and transparent to your stakeholders and to the vendors

4. Find a reliable reference when you report savings like historic data or well established published references.

5. Get the tools of the trade: e-sourcing, spend analysis and contract management. They will make your life easier and your turnaround time shorter.

Don´t:

6. Don´t go into a negotiation table by yourself. Bring at least a team of two and have all team members informed and coordinated.

7. Don´t forget procurement is a function that adds value to the organization not just savings.

8. Don´t treat a vendor or contractor as the opposition or

an enemy, treat them more as a partner in business.

9. If you don´t have enough information go back and get informed. Time is not an excuse for poor judgment.

10. Don´t settle for less. Don´t award a negotiation based on irrelevant factors. Partner with your vendor and get the most out of the relationship together.

Very basic but yet very powerful if they are not neglected. If you feel motivated I encourage you to think on how this applies to your everyday procurement activities and implement.

Also I encourage you to think of the many more practices you can include in your procurement team and your business or your organization.

WHAT'S NEXT FOR STRATEGIC SOURCING AND PROCUREMENT?

First we discover that many process can be expedited and well documented with "made to order" software. The e-sourcing era began, everything got loaded in very nicely crafted software that can go from P2P to RFx, and from Online Bidding to contract management and so on. Then it all started to move to the cloud.

In another front the sourcing process got review improved updated and even pumped up. We moved very swiftly from the common everyday transactional purchasing to an advanced strategic sourcing, contracting and procurement. So good that it became a competitive advantage in many industries!

We got the process right with nice e-sourcing tools, we got the strategy in, and the contracts managed so where are we going from there? If you look into a company that is new to strategic sourcing and procurement, and it is in its first stages where bottom line impact savings are all over and nicely in a double digit arena. As this company matures it´s sourcing the savings decrease and the lemons run out of juice.

What next then? Well now the early adopters of the strategic sourcing and procurement are facing a drought on bottom line savings. What is next? Now is time for collaboration. Supplier – buyer collaboration that is. The next move beyond crafty e-sourcing software and bare savings strategy is collaboration.

Only the collaboration with vendors can bring that next step. When you partner with your vendor you can get ahead of the game. The vendor can share their aches and pains, their drivers, their business model, trends and future plans, at the end they become yours too. The innovation game begins and you are first in line when you collaborate with your vendor. It´s their job to innovate and they need to innovate for you as a customer so collaboration is the key.

Strategic sourcing and procurement is moving forward from strategic to strategic-collaborative-innovative.
Take this into account for your future plans if you wish to get a competitive advantage in a fierce twenty first century market!

ABOUT THE AUTHOR

Bruno Alvarez Born in Guatemala, Central America is regarded in Latin America and the Americas as one of the Leading Contracting and Procurement Expert. He has worked as a full time employee, for global "Fortune 500" companies. He has become the leading voice on contracting excellence based on real life experience in tough market. His international experience is second to none. Develop contracting and execution excellence of large capital projects on the most complex markets such as Latin America and at the same time the world´s largest projects in North America. Have contracted and executed in more than 21 Countries such as:

Argentina, Brazil, Canada, Chile, Colombia, Costa Rica, Dominican Republic, Ecuador, El Salvador, Guatemala, Honduras, Mexico,

Nicaragua, Panama, Peru, Puerto Rico, Surinam, Trinidad and Tobago, Tortola, St. Lucia, United States and others.

Studied at a German Elementary School later to move to Miami Florida, Unites States to get his High school diploma and be regarded as one of the top 100 Outstanding High school Students of America by the US board of education. Moved on to become a Chemical Engineer and later on, professor of Thermodynamics and Physical Chemistry at Universidad del Valle, the best ranked Scientific University in Latin America. Moved on to get a post graduate degree on Business Management and have spent most of the professional life learning and practicing the latest concepts on Contracting and procurement and the advanced contract models in the Energy and Gas Industry.

For lectures, workshops and guest speaker appearances contact:

bruno.a.alvarez@gmail.com